How to Build a Mash-Tun

Bill Owens
Founder of Buffalo Bill's Brewery & The American Distilling Institute

Additional Material From
Ty Phelps, Andalusia Whiskey
& Matt Strickland, Iron City Distilling

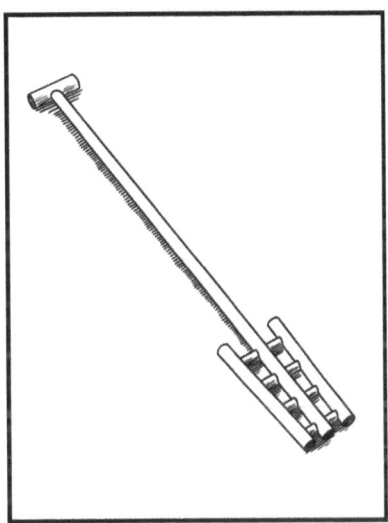

Antique Mash Paddle

Illustrations by Francesca Cosanti
Design by Kate Jordahl

White Mule Publishing
American Distilling Institute

Bill Owens, Buffalo Bill's Brewery, 1983

PREFACE

In the 1970s I was a home brewer and using malt syrup I fermented "beer" in a five gallon bucket. One summer I took a brewing course from Dr. Michael Lewis at UC Davis and learned that barley starches conversion to sugars occurs at 152 degrees. I also read the *Big Book of Brewing* by David Line. The book had illustrations and discussed the all-grain brewing process.

I decided to build my own 10 gallon brewing system. To do so, I bought a 100 quart Coleman camping cooler and installed a slotted copper pipe creating a false bottom. My kettle was made from a Budweiser keg.

I was on my way to opening Buffalo Bills Brewery and years later founding the American Distilling Institute.

In the Spring of 1978, California laws changed, allowing a small brewery to exist.

In 1982, I visited numerous salvage yards, looking for used dairy tanks that I could convert into a mash-tun or a brewing kettle.

In the fall of 1983, I opened Buffalo Bill's Brewery in Hayward, California. The total cost of the equipment, mash-tun, kettle and three fermentation tanks, was less than $10,000. Today, there are over 20,000 craft distillers in the USA, and finding used tanks is very difficult. Craft brewers and distillers are now using stainless steel Intermediate Bulk Containers totes (IBC) and converting them into mash-tuns, kettles, and fermentation vessels.

In 1997, I sold Buffalo Bill's brewery and founded the American Distilling Institute. I'm proud to say two of my labels, *Alimony Ale*, "The Bitterest Beer in America," and *Pumpkin Ale* and my archive about Buffalo Bill's are at the Smithsonian Institute in Washington, D.C.

Bill Owens
Hayward, California

IBC Tote vs. Commercial Mash-Tun

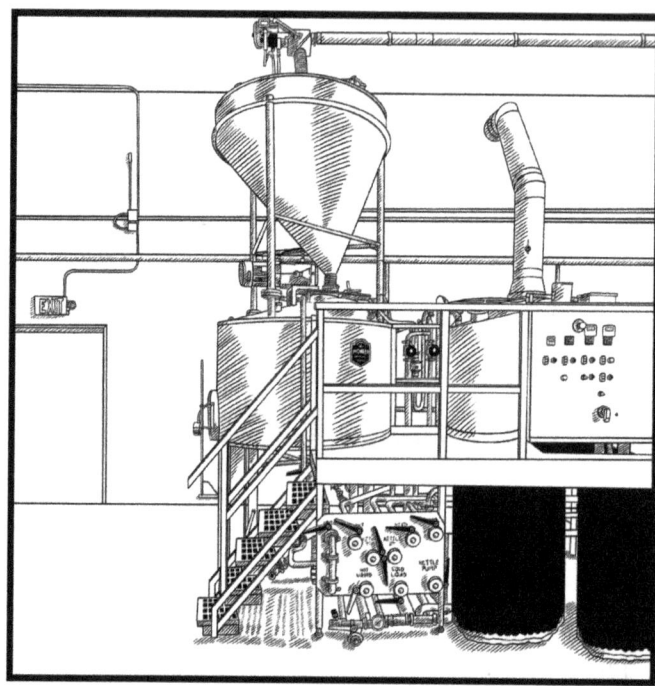

Modern Mash-Tun system makes wash and wort for distilling

Items to Buy

IBC Tote	$6,000
Roller Mill	$8,000
Grain Silo	$7,000
Water Heaters	$4,000
V-Wire Screen	$500
Hydrator	$350
Miscellaneous hoses and valves	$4,000
Welding Shop	$5,000 to $10,000
Anton Paar Handheld Meters	
Density Meter DMA 35 Basic	$3,000
Alcohol Meter: SNAP	$2,000

A mash-tun costs $30,000-$60,000
A steam boiler adds $40,000
Commercial Mash-Tun Total: $100,000

Build your own mash-tun for $30,000

CONVERT THE IBC TOTE TANK INTO A MASH-TUN

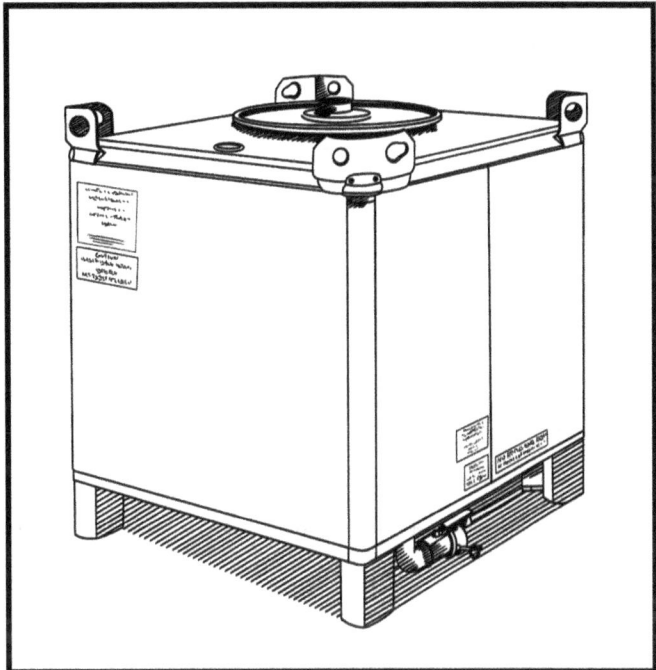

IBC Tote is the backbone of the Craft Distilling Industry.

1. Go to eBay and buy a new or used 350-gallon IBC stainless steel tote tank. Make sure it has a 24-inch lid with a 4-inch porthole. A new tote will run about $4,000. A used IBC tote on eBay will sell for about $1,250.

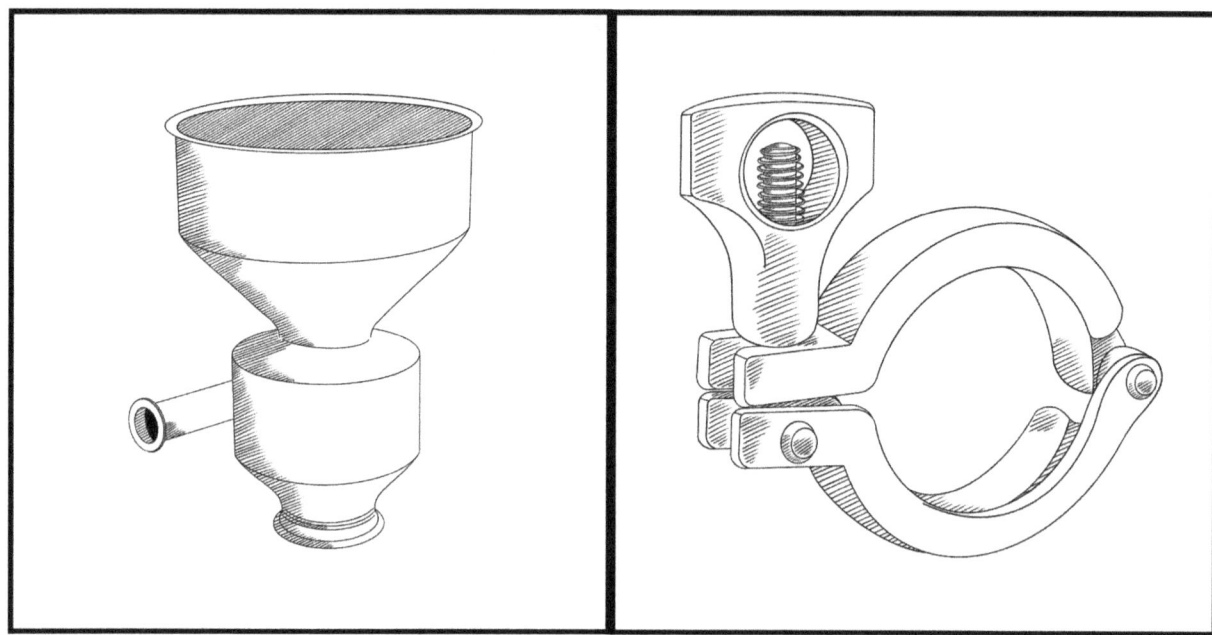

Hydrator and Tri-Clamp

2. Buy two flex augers. One auger delivers grain from the silo to the mill. The other is a flex auger. It transfers milled grain to the hydrator. Two augers cost about $5,000.

3. Buy or rent a grain silo. Many grain companies supply augers and spent-grain dumpsters. To save money, you can skip buying a silo and pour the bags of grain directly into the mill. Silos range from $10,000 to $20,000.

4. Purchase.

   a. One 4-inch tri-clamp. Use it to attach the hydrator to the 4-inch porthole.

   b. One 1.5-inch tri-clamp. Attach the hydrator to the pipe from the water heater

   c. One 10-to-12-inch tri-clamp. Attach the flex auger to the hydrator.

5. Buy a 4-6 grain roller mill that is capable of producing 3,000 lbs. of grist per hour. A good source of mills and augers is www.malthanding.com. Mills run $8,000-$20,000. Do not use a hammer mill to create a grist.

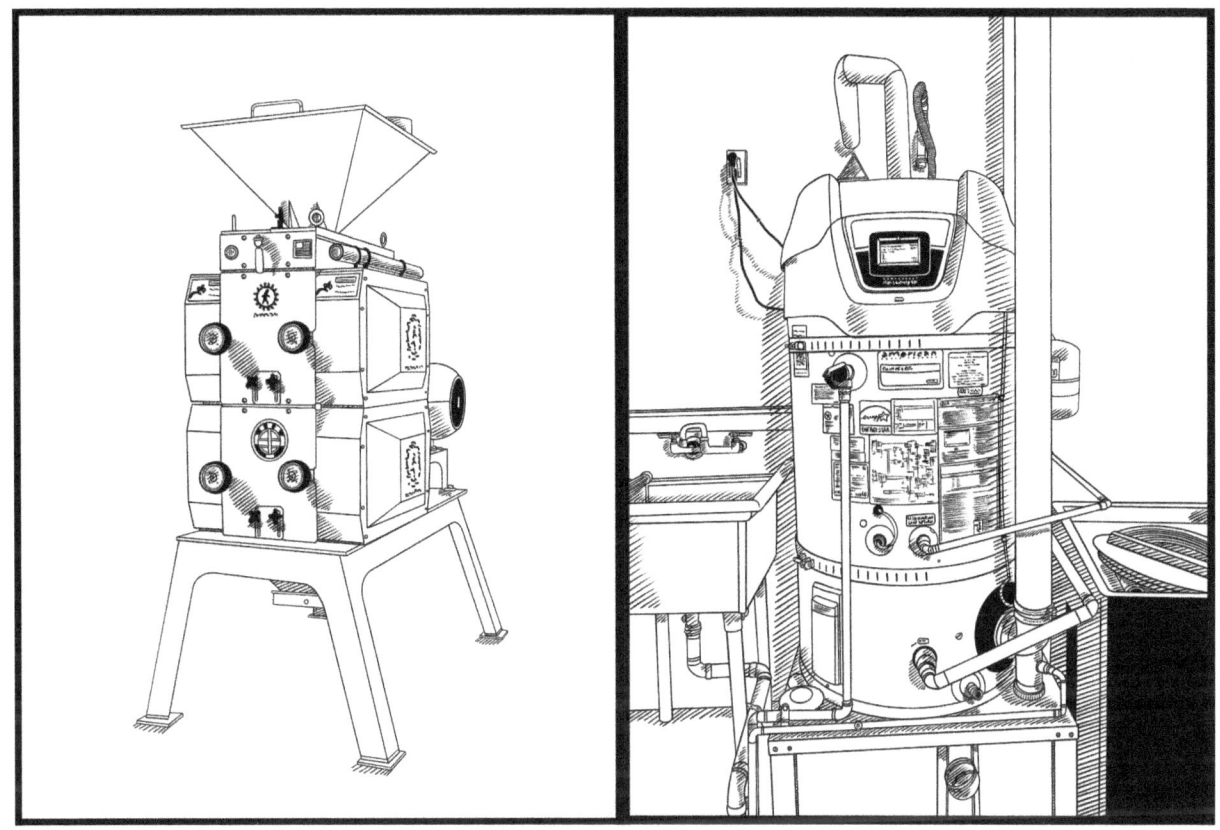

Roller Mill and Water Heater

6. Buy two commercial water heaters or a flash heater that can deliver 400 gallons of "strike water." This eliminates the need to buy a gas steam boiler. Water heaters start at $2,000. *If you buy a direct fire pot kettle you totally eliminate the steam boiler from the distillery saving tens of thousands of dollars.*
7. Buy a heavy-duty workbench with a 3-step ladder. Use the bench as a platform, giving you a place to stand while accessing the mash-tun. Don't use an aluminum ladder in the distillery; instead, build access platforms to the mash-tun and fermentation tanks. A workbench at Harbor Freight costs about $250.00.
8. Purchase a 17x21 inch tank manway and extra door gasket. A manway costs $300 to $800.

IBC Conversion

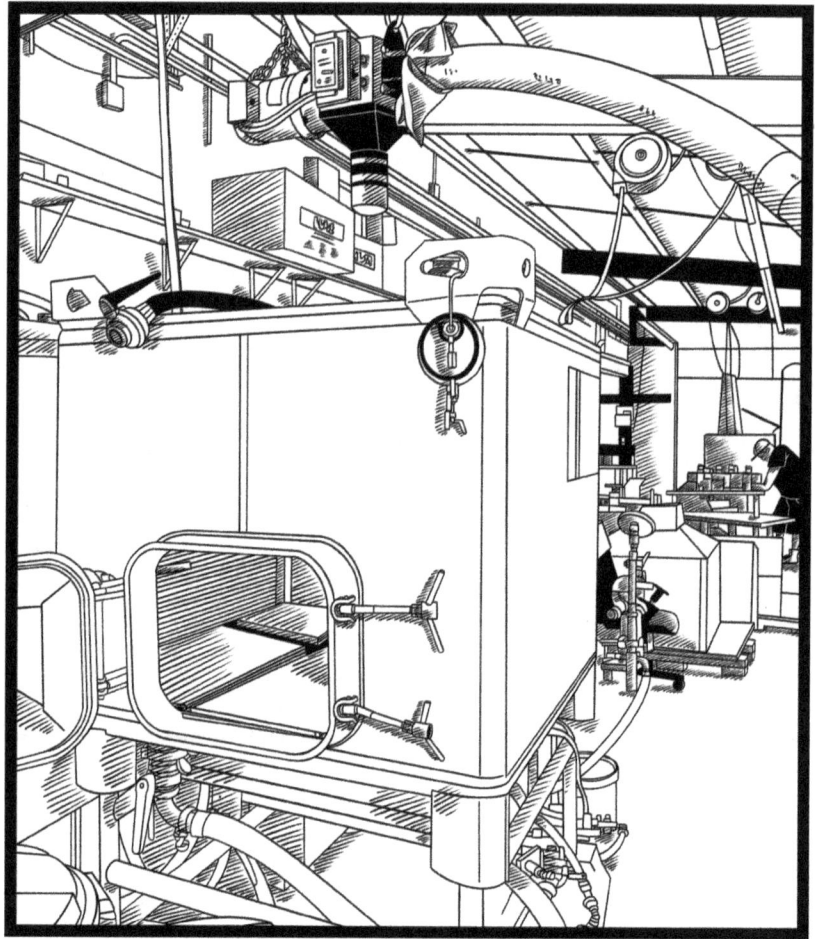

IBC Converted into a Mash-Tun

1. Visit nearby breweries and make friends with the brewers. Tell him or her you are building a whiskey distillery and converting an IBC tote into mash-tun.
2. Ask to photograph their mash-tun, saying you need images of the V-wires screen and false bottom to show your welder. Photograph the handle on the screens. They allow you to pick up and remove the screen for cleaning

Note: the lip under the door aids in the dig-out of the mash-tun

3. Have the tote delivered to a welding shop and have them do the following:

   a. Cut a 14x12x20 inch bean-shaped hole into the top of the tote. Use the hole to gain access to check mash-in and sparging temperatures. The bean hole also allows you to reach in and with a stiff brush, clean the mash-tun. No harsh chemicals are needed to clean a mash-tun, just elbow grease.

   b. In the side of the tote, cut a 12x17 inch hole and install the manway door that gives you access to dig out the spent grains. Use the manway access to install the V-wire screen, creating the false bottom.

Adding a motorized rake for mashing and grain removal is expensive.

c. Cut the V-Screen in sections so that it can be removed through the manway.

d. The height of the legs on the bottom of the tote depends on the grain bins. They should fit under the manway door. You can find bins at www.uline.com

e. On the top of the tote, install a 2/3 inch stainless steel union. To it, attach a ball valve and a pipe running from the water heater. On the lower end of the union, attach the sparging arm. It's constructed from 1/2 inch copper pipe drilled with a row of 1/32 inch holes. When the ball valve is opened it will spray 170-degree water onto the grain bed.

f. Into the bottom of the mash-tun, install a second 2/3 inch union. It should be flush with the bottom of the tun. Attach a ball valve to the union. When the valve is opened, the wort will flow into a collection tub.

Building a platform for your mash-tun will give you a place to work vs. a dangerous ladder

LOGBOOK
Suggestions for a weekly mashing schedule

DAY ONE: Monday	Mashing and fermentation.
*DAY TWO: Tuesday	Mashing and fermentation
DAY THREE: Wednesday	Mashing and fermentation.
DAY FOUR: Thursday	Do the spirits run from the previous week's fermentations
DAY FIVE: Friday	Blend together Monday, Tuesday and Wednesday fermentations.
DAY SIX: Saturday	Do a stripping run, turning the 8% beer into 40% alcohol called low wines.
DAY SEVEN: Sunday	Day of rest.
DAY EIGHT: Monday	Make the spirits run, distilling 40% *low wines* to 128 proof called *new make whiskey*. Age the new make whiskey in new charred American oak barrels for one year. *Some people water the 128 proof to 100 proof and without aging it bottle and sell it as moonshine.*

* Using a 350 gallon tote and a hydrator you can to do two mashes a day producing 700 gallons of sweet wort.

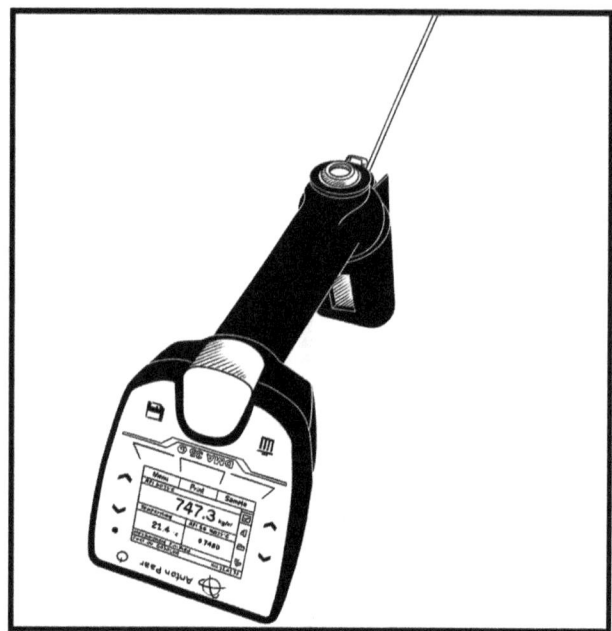

Anton Paar handheld alcohol meter: SNAP

MASHING-IN

7 A.M. Pre-heat the tun. Turn on the water heaters, dropping 10-15 gallons of 170-degree water into the bottom of the tub. Drain the water

1. THE MILLING and AUGERING

    a. Turn on the auger, feeding the grain from the silo to the mill.

    b. Turn on the mill, feeding the grist into the hopper.

    c. Turn on the flex auger feeding the grist into the hydrator.

2. STRIKING OR MASHING-IN

    a. Turn on the 170 degree hot water tank feeding the mash-tun for 10-20 seconds

    b. Turn on the grain feed to the Hydrator. As the grain and hot water mix it forms hot mash.

    The mixing in the hydrator drop the temperature of the mash from 170 degrees to 160 degree. As the mash drops from the hydrator into the bottom of the mash-tun it will lose another 10 degrees. (170 degrees minus 20 degrees equals 150 degrees)

The ideal mash-in temperature should be 152 degrees. The thermal mass of the mash at 152 degrees will hold for 10 to 15 minutes. A double-jacketed insulated mash-tun is not necessary. In 10 minutes, starch conversion is done. Two-row American barley is highly modified, and according to barley experts, the conversion of barley starched into sugars takes only minutes.

D. It takes about 15 minutes for the hydrator to mix 900 lbs. of grain with 300 gallons of water producing the mash bed. The thickness of the mash is like One-minute Quaker Oats.

E. Sometimes during the mashing in process, lumps of grain will form. If so use a mash paddle and break up the lumps. If you are planning a large mash-tun holding over 1,000 pounds of grain, I suggest adding motorized rakes to the system. The rakes can also be used for cleaning out the mash-tun and pushing the spent grain into waiting bins. Motorized rakes add thousands of dollars to the cost of building a mash-tun.

F. Use an infrared thermometer gun to check and record the temperature of the mash.

If you screwed up and mashed-in at 140 or 170 degrees don't worry. I can assure you the barley enzymes are very forgiving, and most of the starches will have converted to sugars. You have produced a low 5% or high 8% alcohol wort. Ferment and distill it.

Sparging Process

1. After mashing-in, wait 10 minutes for the starch-to-sugar conversion to be complete.
2. Turn on the valve from the water heater to the sparging arm.
3. The sparging challenge is to keep the grain bed floating. To do this the sparge water flowing on to the grain bed should be the same volume as the wort running into the collection tub. If you run the wort too fast the grain bed will collapse. Do not stir the bed. After sparging for a few minutes, the grain bed will settle to the bottom of the tun. Craft distillers as a rule sparge very little as they want to produce high alcohol beer.
4. The wort is flowing into a collection tub. When the tub is full pump it onto a heat exchanger. A fermentation temperature of 70 degrees is ideal.
5. Most distillers use dry yeast. I prefer to pitch yeast from a previous fermentation. As a brewer, I often went 20 to 30 generations before going back to dry yeast.
6. Do not allow a dirty mash-tun to set overnight, as it will attract mice.
7. Keep a record of the process. Whiskeyresources.com sells a good record keeping program for both large and small distilleries.

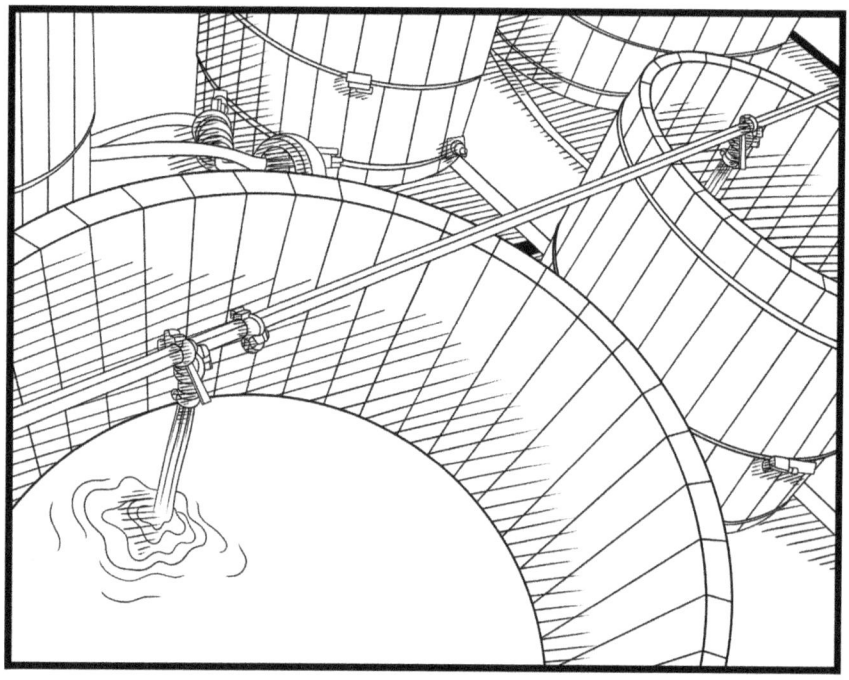

Wooden Fermenters at Leopold's Brothers, Denver, Colorado

RUNNING THE WORT

Open the ball valve and catch the first half pint of wort draining from the mash-tun. It will be cloudy. I use a small container to catch and toss it back onto the mash bed. A half-pint of cloudy wort is not going to affect flavor. Many brewers and distillers pump the cloudy wash back onto the mash bed. Using a pump to recycle such a small amount of wort is a waste of time.

As the wort flows you will see that the mash bed is starting to settle. Do not stir the mash bed. If you do the bed will collapse, slowing down the flow of the wort to the collection tub. When you have finished collecting the wort move the drain valve pipe to a second tub. Allow the grain bed to drain or rest for one hour. Dry grain is easy to dig-out.

Sparging is a balancing act. I call it "slipping and sliding". You slip wort out from the bottom of the tun while sliding (spraying) water onto the grain bed. Sparging or rinsing removes any remaining sugar from the grain bed. If you want a high gravity wort, sparge very little. I suggest doing a high gravity wort, for example an old school barley wine recipe, giving you a richer tasting whiskey.

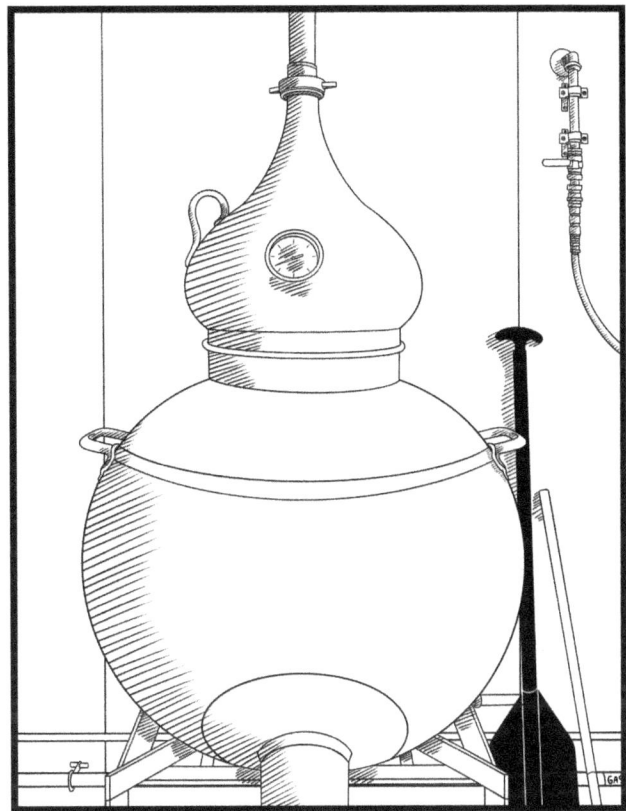

Hoga direct fire still at The Orkney Distillery, Scotland

Pot Distilling Process

1. Using a 250-gallon direct-fire pot still, make four stripping runs. Each run produces 55 gallons of low wines at 65 proofs. Combine the four runs, distilling it from 65 to 128 proof.
3. Whiskey and water don't mix well. Take several day to proof it down for bottling
4. Annual production using a 250-gallon pot still and a hydrator mashing system is 200 barrels which will make 4,000 9-liter cases.
5. The price per bottle is $36. Enjoy.

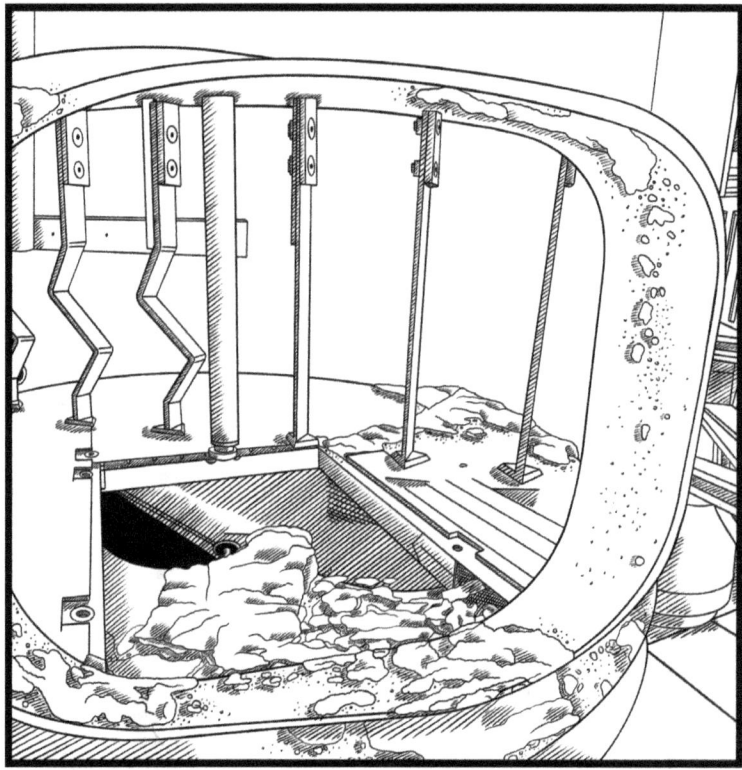

Mash-tun with a section of the V-wire removed for cleaning

NOTES ON MASHING AND FERMENTATION

1. Once a week take apart and clean heat exchanger. At the beginning this process is very intimidating as it is easy to get the plates mixed up.
2. Make your own digital film showing how to clean your heat exchanger so you can put it back together. On Goggle, search "How to clean a plate and frame heat exchanger."
3. After filling the fermentation tank, use an Anton Paar Handheld Density Meter DMA 35 to record the gravity of the wort. The original gravity should be around 1060. After a 3-day fermentation the final gravity should be around 1010. If so, you have produced an 8% beer wash ready for the stripping run.

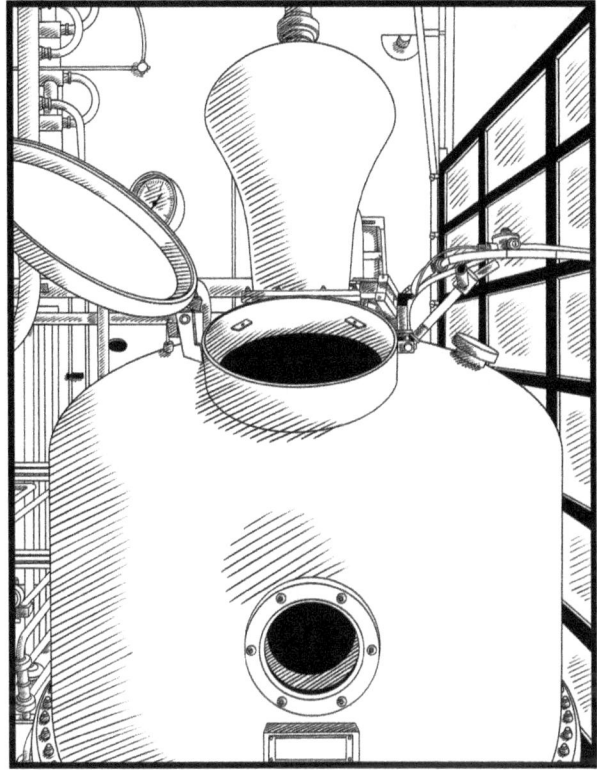

Vendome Copper Whiskey Pot Still

4. Old-fashioned floating hydrometers are inaccurate and difficult to work with. A density meter is worth every penny. An Anton Paar density meter costs about $3,000.
5. Today, most craft distillers use open top IBC totes as fermenters because they are easy to clean. Some distillers are using wooden fermentation tanks. Visit the American Distilling Institute Forums at https://adiforums.com for more information.
6. Do not allow a dirty mash-tun to sit overnight, as it will attract mice.

Final Thoughts: Why Malt Whiskey?

The mash-tun is the backbone of a single malt whiskey distilling. American barley is loaded with natural enzymes that in a matter of minutes convert starches into sugars. Malt whiskey aged in a new American oak barrel in less than a year will be ready to drink. American white oak (Quercus alba) has wonderful vanilla notes similar to vanilla ice cream. Don't age American single malt whiskey in French (Quercus robur) wine barrels.

Corn whiskey should be aged two years and gets 60% of its flavor from the barrel. I have never distilled corn whiskey because it requires a steam boiler, corn cooker and a different mash separation system. The production a corn whiskey can add 4-6 hours to the brew day. Corn mash also requires the use of commercial enzymes to convert the corn starches into fermentable sugars.

The process of making single malt whiskeys is simple and does not require steam boilers or use of enzymes for starch conversion.

With the iPhones and computers we live in the world where there is not much physical work to be done. Many small brewers/distilleries are already almost fully automated. To mash-in, they just push a button on the computer screen.

At a small brewpub or craft distillery, there is actual physical work. It ranges from lifting 50 lbs. of grain for the mill or digging out the mash-tun. You can actually break a bead of sweat digging out a mash-tun.

This book is a celebration of going back to basic and doing the physical work of "mashing-in" and "digging out" the mash-tun. It's a job that produces a real product, beer and spirits. In 14 years as a brewer I dug out the mash-tun 648 times and at the age of 85 feel hard work is good for you. I don't drink water from plastic bottles.

Bill Owens
Hayward, California

Images on next page: Top left is of 1700's farm distillery mash-tun. The false bottom is a wood box attached to the side of the barrel. After mashing-in the box becomes the false bottom and the small holes in the box provide a path way for the wort to drain. The image bottom left is a home brewers mash-tun made from a camping cooler. After mashing in the slotted copper pipe provide a path to drain the wort.

Home Brewing and Historical Mashing

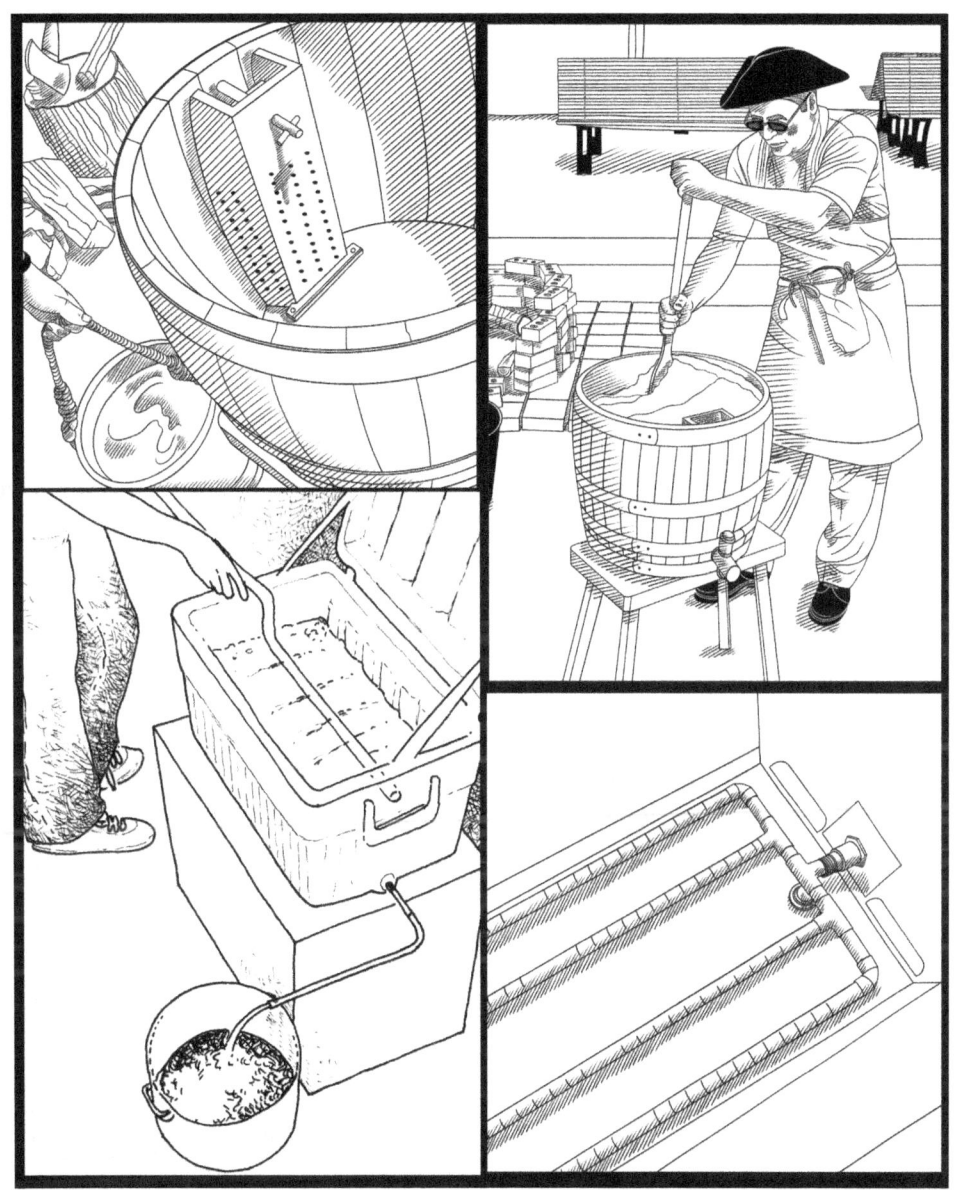

Mash Chemistry 101
by Matt Strickland

Sometimes it's good to go back to the basics. A refresher on a seemingly familiar topic can be … well, refreshing.

Mash chemistry is one of those topics that a lot of folks feel like they have a solid handle on. Seems easy doesn't it? Take starch-heavy grain, apply heat and water, infuse with a little patience and you should have yourself a fermentable sugar profile that your yeast can produce alcohol from.

If this all sounds simple that's because on the surface it is. Of course, this seeming simplicity obscures a complicated set of chemical reactions worthy of a deeper understanding. Let's take a look at mashing chemistry and what actually happens under the liquid hood. For some people this may be a bit of a refresher, but the goal is that you walk away with a more refined understanding of mashing principles. For others this material may feel entirely new and hopefully you'll feel that much more confident when it comes time to tackle the mysteries of grain to glass. So, let's dive in, shall we?

The Problem of Starch

Why can't we simply take milled wet grain, add yeast and get alcohol? Hell, it works just fine with grapes and honey. Shouldn't we be able to do the same thing with our barley and corn? That'd be nice, but unfortunately things just don't work that way. The reason is that while grapes are composed of simple fermentable sugars, grains are composed of starch.

As far as the plant is concerned, starch is not there for us to reap its alcohol-producing potential. To the plant, starch serves as a form of energy storage that the embryo plant can use when it starts to germinate. Of course, we're human beings, dammit, and there's very little on this earth that someone hasn't tried to ferment and get a buzz off of. At some point in our history of drunken befuddlement someone figured out that, if you add water and the right amount of heat to grain, the resulting liquid will taste sweet. Turn a few centuries' worth of pages and we've realized that yeast exists to consume sugars from sweet-tasting things (including mashed grain) and produce alcohol as a by-product.

To understand how mashing works, it helps to take a closer look at what the inside of a grain kernel looks like. Figure 1 shows an anatomical drawing of a barley kernel. Don't worry if you

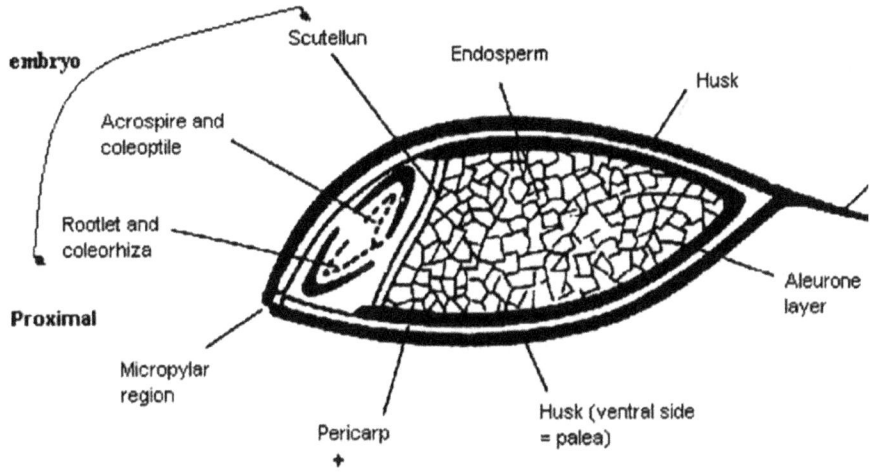

Fig. 1: Barley kernel structure

use other grains instead of barley; many (but not all) of the structures of barley hold true for the other common whiskey grains. Note the large area taken up by the endosperm: This is where the starch is held.

Endosperm starch is bound up into microscopic granules. Different grains have different sizes and shapes of granules. In barley there are two types of starch granules, both basically spherical in shape. Type A granules are the larger of the two, usually about 20 μm in size. Type B granules are much smaller, generally ranging from 3–10 μm.

Now why is this important? In order for our mash to be successful we need water (we'll see exactly why later) to be able to penetrate the inner depths of the starch granule to unfold and gelatinize it. Smaller granules are more compact than their bigger brothers and therefore don't allow water to flow through quite as easily. This is why corn typically requires more energy to mash than other grains. Corn starch is primarily made up of smaller compact starch granules, making their gelatinization more difficult.

So, we know that we need to gelatinize the starch granules, essentially opening them up with water and forming a gel. The reason for that is we want better access to what composes the starch. Grain starch is composed of glucose molecules bound together in chains. These grain starch chains come in two types: amylose and amylopectin. Amylose is essentially a straight chain of glucose molecules, not too complicated, but it has the ability to form pretty dense starch granules, particularly in some varieties of corn. Amylopectin has a branched structure of glucose strands and for many grains makes up about 75% of the total starch content (see Fig. 2).

In Figure 2, it's important to note the "branch point" is based on an α(1,6) bond. It's not important to understand the chemical nature of that type of bond, just that it exists and that it presents some challenges. We'll explain in a bit.

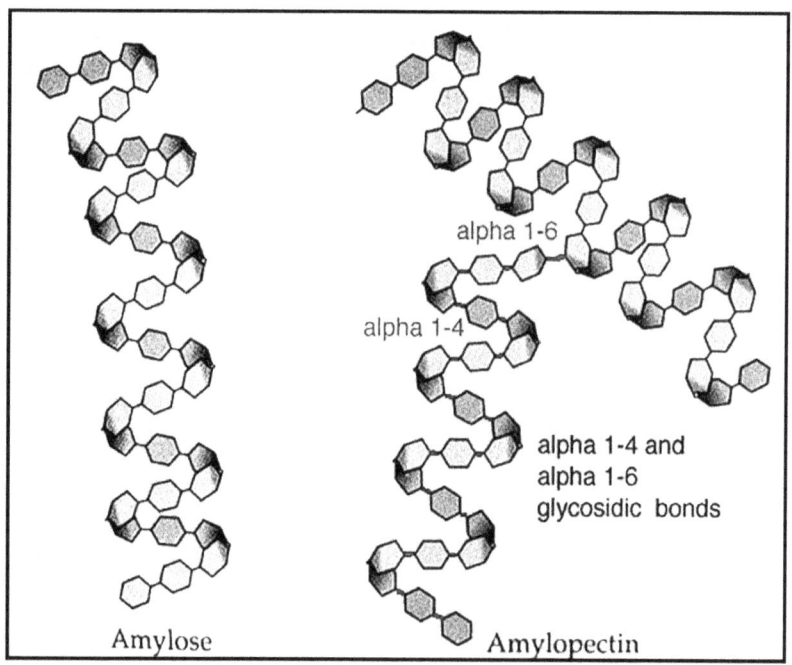

Fig. 2: Amylose structure vs Amylopectin

Look at all those glucose molecules. Pretty sexy, right? They are if you're a yeast cell. Yeast makes alcohol by consuming sugar and metabolizing it. Glucose is a sugar. So is maltose, which is two glucose molecules bound together. Fructose and sucrose? Yep: sugars. We want to break those starch molecules of amylose and amylopectin chains down into simpler molecules for yeast consumption. That, my friends, is the primary purpose of mashing.

Sounds great. How do we do that, though?

Accessing the Sugars in Starch

We've already established that we need water, and you may have already deduced that we need heat as well. How about adding some hot water, then? That should do the trick.

If we add hot water to our milled grain (the type, consistency and process of milling is another story entirely), then that water should be able to penetrate the starch granules, opening them up to expose the starch chains. However, heat and water do not break down starch into simpler sugars — not on their own, anyway. In order to do that we need enzymes.

The important enzymes for barley are developed during malting. Contrary to popular explanations on the subject, there are actually quite a few enzymes at play during the whiskey mashing process. The ones that get talked about the most are the amylases, both alpha (α) and beta (β). Make no mistake: These are important components of our mashing system. Amylases are responsible for breaking apart much of our starch molecules into the simpler sugars we're after.

Alpha-amylase behaves like the clumsy brute of the two. It works best at higher temperatures (optimum activity occurs between 66–71° C [150–160°F]) than β-amylase. It is also what we call a "liquefaction" enzyme because it quickly gelatinizes our starch granules. You can actually watch this process happen. Try mashing unmalted wheat or rye by itself and you'll notice that the overall mixture is incredibly gummy and viscous. Add in 5–10% by total grist weight of malted barley and you'll see the viscosity of your mash magically get thinner and easier to handle.

Alpha-amylase is what we call an "endo-amylase," meaning it tends to clip starch chains at points in the middle of the chain. This is a fairly random process for α-amylase, but it goes a long way toward reducing the mash viscosity brought on by pasty starch granules. This also means that α-amylase is not really our champion when it comes to producing fermentable sugar from starch. Small amounts of sugars are produced at so random a pace that it just isn't realistic to rely on α-amylase to give us every sugar we're looking for.

For that we need β-amylase. Beta-amylase works at lower temperatures than its hot-headed brother, generally 54–66° C (129–150°F), with the highest activity seen around 64 (147°F). Beta-amylase is an "exo-amylase," which means it attacks starch chains from their ends and works its way along the chain in a methodical and linear fashion. It breaks off one molecule of maltose (a two-glucose molecule) at a time.

Amylose is easily handled by both amylases working in concert with each other. After all, amylose is essentially a straight chain of glucose molecules, so α-amylase and β-amylase have no issues with converting it to simpler sugars.

Amylopectin, with its myriad of branch points, is another story entirely. Beta-amylase moves along the amylopectin chains until it gets within two or three glucose units of an α(1,6) branch point before it has to abandon ship and move on to another less-encumbered starch chain. But remember, these branch points are also composed of glucose molecules, so we don't want to leave them alone.

So how do we break down the branch points and increase our overall wort fermentability? This is where our secondary enzymes come into play. Limit dextrinase (sometimes referred to as pullulanase) has the ability to break apart α(1,6) bonds. Amyloglucosidase breaks down larger sugars like maltotetrose (a four-glucose molecule) and maltotriose (a three-glucose molecule) down into singular glucose molecules (See Fig. 3).

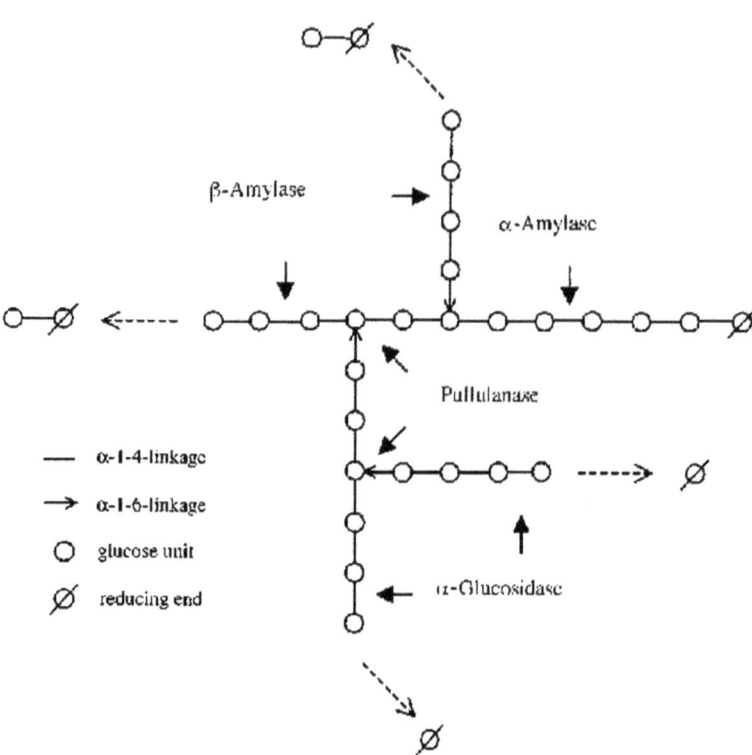

Fig. 3: Actions of mash enzymes

But here's the catch with these secondary enzymes: Compared to their amylase cousins, they aren't very active during normal mashing conditions. However, they do become more active during fermentation and give us what we call a "secondary conversion." This secondary conversion actually increases the amount of fermentable sugars by upward of 15%, which is a huge boost to our plant efficiency. Brewers boil their wort after mashing to sanitize it and for hop utilization (among other things), which denatures all the mash enzymes, especially our secondary enzymes. Since distillers typically don't boil their wort, we get to keep these valuable enzymes in play for more starch conversion to take place (see Fig. 3).

What You Need to Know About Water

We've talked about starch and the enzymes to break it down into fermentable extract, but we've only danced around the factors that make those enzymes active. Clearly, we need water, as it is required to penetrate the starch granules. Heat added to the water aids in gelatinizing the starch and as we mentioned a moment ago, our amylases have preferred temperature ranges. So, what's the correct mash temperature for grain spirits production?

The answer (sort of) depends. First off, what we're talking about here is "saccharification" temperature, which is where our amylases do their jobs. In that case we want to think about what each amylase is doing. Generally, for distilling purposes, we're interested in obtaining the most fermentable wort possible. For that, β-amylase is our guy and has an optimum activity at 64° C (147°F). Notice that this falls just shy of our preferred temperature range for α-amylase activity, but that's OK here. Alpha-amylase still works suitably well at 64° C, breaking apart starch chains and making them more easily attackable by β-amylase.

Next to the temperature of the water, we have to talk about the amount of water. This is essentially a question of mash thickness. There are pros and cons for thin mashes (lots of water) to thick mashes (less water). Thin mashes are much easier to work with than thicker mashes, as they have more water to aid in the movement of grain solids from place to place. The drawback is that with thin mashes you have to be much more careful with monitoring your mash temperature. Thin mashes don't provide much in the way of insulation for enzymes, and small changes in mash temperature can have dramatic effects on enzyme performance. These concepts work the opposite way for thick mashes: more enzyme heat insulation but harder to work with. So, what's the sweet spot? It depends on who you talk to since every system, distiller and recipe is a little bit different. However, 1.5 quarts of water per pound of grain works well for most folks. (In metric, you're looking at roughly 3 liters of water per kilogram of grain.)

The other key parameter at play that we haven't discussed is mash pH. The pH of a system is simply a way to measure how acidic or basic the system is. Mash pH is incredibly important for enzyme activity. Without getting into the chemistry too much, pH affects the shape of the enzymes that we care about. If the pH isn't within a suitable range, our amylases and secondary enzymes won't function well and, in some cases, not at all. The accepted pH range for mashing is 5.2–5.8, with 5.4 considered the optimum. Above this range and starch conversion will still occur but at a significantly slower pace. Below 5.0, the amylase enzymes stop working altogether.

Finally, we need to discuss how long the mash should take. Once again, this depends on what you're talking about when it comes to "mashing," which for the moment is simply the saccharification step. The amount of time needed for conversion is affected by several factors that get too complicated to discuss in detail here. Things like mash thickness, temperature, pH, recipe composition and malt modification all play a role. However, let's keep things simple. In general, a saccharification rest should last anywhere from 30 minutes for high amounts of malted grains in the recipe to 60 minutes for low amounts of malted grains. See Table 1 for a handy summary of all these factors.

Condition	Low	Optimum	High
Temperature.	Low temperatures do not affect the enzymes much, but the starch must be gelatinised first to achieve quick conversion. Gelatinisation temperature for malt starch is 60-65°C.	65°C	High temperatures inactivate enzymes, including α and β amylases and limit dextrinase. The action of amylases is stopped at temperatures over 70°C.
pH.	Acidic conditions kill the enzymes. Enzyme action is stopped at pHs below 5.0	5.4	High pHs slow enzyme action, but it does continue at pHs of 7 or above.
Water. (Mash thickness)	Enzymes are more sensitive to heat in a thin mash. There is a lower concentration of enzyme and starch in a thin mash.	Between 2.5 and 3.5 litres of water per kilogram of dry grist.	Enzymes are less sensitive to heat in a thick mash. There is a higher concentration of enzyme and starch in a thick mash.
Time.	Enzymes take time to attack the starch. Conversion will be incomplete in less than 30 minutes.	30 minutes	Conversion will be almost complete after 30 minutes. A longer time will not increase the yield of sugar but may make it more fermentable, but not if the temperature is ~65°C.

Table 1: Summary of factors affecting amylase enzyme performance.
From Whisky: Technology, Production, and Marketing, ed. Inge Russell, 2003.

Getting Sugar from Other Grains

Up to this point we've really only talked about mashes with high amounts of barley in them, which excluding the burgeoning American single malt whiskey category is not that common in the United States. What if we're making a high-corn bourbon or rye whiskey? How does the mash chemistry work in those systems? These types of whiskeys have large amounts of unmalted or "adjunct" grains in them, which does change the processing steps a little bit.

Fortunately for us, the primary objectives for mashing unmalted grains are pretty much the same. We have a source of starch that we need to convert into simpler sugars. Unfortunately, because the grain isn't malted, our grains don't have much in the way of saccharification enzymes to help us along. Also, remember what we talked about with starch granules earlier: Not all starch behaves the same way.

First off, different starches require different temperatures to properly gelatinize. Conveniently for brewers using barley, the gelatinization temperature for barley starch is in a similar range to the amylase enzyme activity optimum. However, for corn starch the gelatinization temperature is significantly higher. Corn starch granules are typically small in size (Type B), polyhedral in shape and have low amylopectin contents (see Fig. 4). This makes water penetration into the granule difficult at lower temperatures. Therefore, it is common to see recommended corn starch gelatinization temps of 70–80° C (158–176°F). In practice, however, most corn whiskey distillers will

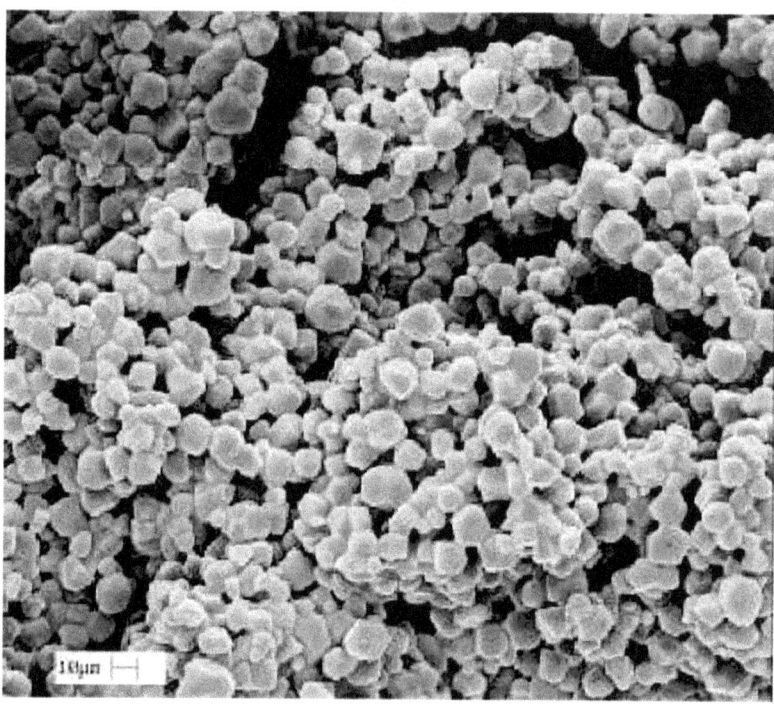

Fig. 4: Micrograph of corn starch granules (1,000X).

tell you that unless you want to wait around all day for your corn to gelatinize, you're better off kicking that temperature up to 90–100° C (194–212°F). For a list of starch gelatinization temperatures see Table 2.

This "cooking" of the grain is obviously energy-intensive. It's therefore not uncommon for distillers to add commercially prepared exogenous enzymes to their mashes to help push things along.

Starch	Gelatinization Temperature Range °C
Barley	52 – 59
Wheat	58 – 64
Rye	57 – 70
Corn (maize)	62 – 72
High amylose corn	67 – 80
Rice	68 – 77
Sorghum	68 – 77
Potato	58 – 68
Tapioca	59 – 69
Sweet Potato	58 – 72

Table 2: Gelatinization temperature ranges for common starch sources.

In the case of corn, there are several high-temperature amylase preparations (typically fungus-derived) that can be dosed into the cooker. Depending on the product this can lead to several benefits. First is the quick reduction of viscosity in the cooker. Second is gelatinizing of starch at lower temperatures, reducing energy needs. However, many bourbon distilleries operate just fine without the addition of enzymes, so it comes down to a matter of preference. Regardless, the cooking of corn generally lasts anywhere from 30–60 minutes depending on the distiller and the specific process they're using. If you're cooking at a higher temperature, then less time is necessary to achieve the desired results.

Note in Table 2 that rye starch has a higher gelatinization temperature range than barley does. There is some overlap there, but rye skews closer to the 70° C (158° F) mark than barley does. At that temp we don't get much in the way of β-amylase activity, so many distillers opt to cook their corn at 70° C (158° F). You might be wondering why they wouldn't just cook it at 90° C (194° F) or higher if they're doing, say, a bourbon with rye. That's a valid point, but there's a problem there. First, adding more grain requires more heat to gelatinize all the starch in the system. Secondly, at least anecdotally, many distillers report that cooking rye at too hot a temperature causes a lot of the natural "gummy" compounds in rye (beta-glucans and arabinoxylans, mostly) to cause problems with mash viscosity. Research on rye viscosity is somewhat scant but what little has been done, does suggest that extraction of arabinoxylans increase with temperature (https://link.springer.com/article/10.1186/s40538-017-0096-6#citeas). Arabinoxylan contents can be reduced somewhat by using malted rye that was put through a long and cool germination period. *(Yujuan Wang, Zhao Jin, et al. "Micro-Malting for the Quality Evaluation of Rye (Secale cereale) Genotypes," Fermentation 2018, 4:50)* However, if you're using malted rye, then you've paid for the enzymes and you wouldn't want to denature them by cooking above 70° C (158° F).

This is why during a mash with unmalted (adjunct) grains, there is generally a step-down cooking process. We start at 90° C (194° F) for corn and sit there for 30 minutes or so. Then we cool down to 70° C (158° F) and add our rye and sit for another 30 minutes before finally cooling to our saccharification temperature of 64° C (147° F).

There's a lot more to cover with mash chemistry, but we've tried to cover the basics here. Hopefully this gives you a better understanding of what's happening in your mash whether you're a bourbon maker or single-malt guru. Better whiskey starts with your materials and your mash technique. Happy brewing!

Annual American Distilling Institute (ADI) Conference. Distilling.com for more information.

ADDITIONAL ADI & BILL OWENS DISTILLING PUBLICATIONS

The American Distilling Institute Coloring Book by Bill Owens
The Nano Distillery: The Future of Distilling compiled by Bill Owens
Modern Moonshine Techniques by Bill Owens
99 Pot Stills by Bill Owens
How to Build a Small Brewery by Bill Owens
Craft of Whiskey Distilling by Bill Owens
Bill Owens' Buffalo Bill's Brewery by Pat Walls
The Delco Years, a dystopian novel by Bill Owens

How to Build a Mash-Tun
Written by Bill Owens

ADDITIONAL MATERIAL
Ty Phelps, Andalusia Whiskey
Matt Strickland, Iron City Distilling

Illustrations by Francesca Cosanti
Designed by Kate Jordahl

Copyright © 2024, White Mule Press
ISBN 978-1-7369802-8-6

To order more copies, contact bill@distilling.com

Distilling.com

www.ingramcontent.com/pod-product-compliance
Lightning Source LLC
Chambersburg PA
CBHW080450110426
42743CB00016B/3337